D0553172

AUTHOR

BEAVER, P

CLASS

623.825

TITLE   039969062

NATO navies of the 1980s

1. Alongside at Portland Naval Base, Great Britain: a Canadian destroyer, a West German destroyer of the *Hamburg* Class and a 'Gun *Leander*' Class frigate (probably *Juno*, the flagship of the Force at the time).

Introduction

Published in 1985 by Arms and Armour Press,
2–6 Hampstead High Street, London NW3 1QQ.

Distributed in the United States by
Sterling Publishing Co. Inc., 2 Park Avenue,
New York, N.Y. 10016.

British Library Cataloguing in Publication Data:
Beaver, Paul
NATO navies of the 1980s. – Warships illustrated; 3)
1. North Atlantic Treaty Organization – Armed
Forces   2. Warships
I. Title   II. Series
623.82′5′091821   VA40
ISBN 0-85368-723-4

Editing, design and artwork by Roger Chesneau.
Typesetting by Typesetters (Birmingham) Ltd.
Printed in Italy by Tipolitografia G. Canale
& C. S.p.A., Turin, in association with Keats
European Ltd.

In the years since the end of the Second World War, Europe and the North Atlantic area, from the Pole to the Tropic of Cancer, have been almost untouched by hostilities. It is no coincidence that this region forms the bulk of the NATO area.

The North Atlantic Treaty Organization, born in 1949, is recognized as a major contributor to the peace of the world, and naval power plays a vital part in the NATO philosophy: two important commands (out of three) are naval – Supreme Allied Commander Atlantic (SACLANT) and Commander-in-Chief Channel (CINCHAN).

In this pictorial guide to the modern combat ships of the Western allies, particular attention has been paid to the smaller nations whose contribution is much valued because it helps to redress the balance of forces so dominated by the Warsaw Pact. Both France and Spain have been included, although they are members outside the actual command structure (except in war), but the coast guard cutters of Iceland have been omitted; Luxembourg, of course, has no navy nor maritime forces. Of the remaining nations, not all the Royal Navy's nor all the United States Navy's warships are assigned to NATO, so the coverage of these services is perhaps less than one would expect.

Each navy has been considered in turn and its range of vessels illustrated, together with the warships which from time to time make up the two NATO Standing Forces, in the Atlantic (STANAVFORLANT) and the Channel (STANAVFORCHAN).

I am indebted to all the member states' Naval Attachés, to the British Naval Attachés in NATO and to the public relations officers of the Commands for their valuable assistance.

Paul Beaver

◀2
2. Standing Naval Force Channel (STANAVFOR-CHAN) normally consists of eight ships, but national commitments may mean that the force is decreased to only five on certain occasions. Here *Bildeston* (RN) keeps the NATO flag flying with *Naaldwijk* (M809) and *Hoogeveen* (M827), both Dutch coastal mine-sweepers; in the centre is the minehunter head-quarters ship, *François Bovesse* (M909) of the Royal Belgian Navy, with *Völkingen* (M1087) bringing up the rear. (RN)

▲3

3. STANAVFORLANT is a force in being: it represents the resolve and co-operation within NATO of the members to defend themselves and each other. Seen off the beautiful Norwegian coast are (left to right) British, West German, Dutch, Canadian (flagship), American and Norwegian escorts. (NATO)

4. NATO has the only multi-national naval escort squadron in a permanent formation anywhere in the world. This is a full squadron, made up of *Rommel* (Federal German Navy, top), *Peder Skram* (Royal Danish Navy), *Comandante João Belo* (Portuguese Navy), *Westhinder* (Royal Belgian Navy), *Comte de Grasse* (US Navy, with *São Gabriel*, PN, centre), *Banckert* (Royal Netherlands Navy), *Narvik* (Royal Norwegian Navy), *Margaree* (Canadian Forces) and *Brazen* (Royal Navy). (NATO)

▼4

5. STANAVFORLANT is part of the NATO subordinate force structure reporting to Supreme Allied Commander Atlantic (SACLANT), at Norfolk, Virginia, USA; this appointment always goes to a US Navy Admiral with a NATO role only. The commander of the Force is always afloat and his warships wear the NATO pennant, as seen in this stern view. The nearest warship is *Trondheim* (F302), of the Royal Norwegian Navy. (NATO)

6. It would not be normal for warships to steam so close together operationally, but these destroyers and frigates of STAN-AVFORLANT are posing for the camera. The vessels are *Skeena* (207, nearest the camera), *Evertsen* (F815), *Braunschweig* (F225, leading), *Aurora* (F10) and *Charles F. Adams* (DDG–2). (USN)

5▲ 6▼

▲7

▲8 ▼9

7. Standing Naval Force Channel (STANAVFOR-CHAN) is the second multi-national force which has warships permanently assigned to it by member nations, who rotate the command. The senior officer of Force is always afloat, reporting, as a NATO subordinate commander, to Commander-in-Chief Channel, who is always the British Commander-in-Chief Fleet (CINCFLEET), with his headquarters at Northwood. Here *Bildeston* (M1110), bottom right, leads a West German, a Belgian and two Dutch MCMVs (mines countermeasures vessels). The destruction of enemy mines is the prime purpose of STANAVFORCHAN in time of war. (RN)

8. The full force turns out for a change of command, which happens regularly, almost yearly. Here, at Zeebrugge in 1983, a Belgian officer takes over from a West German commander. Closest to the camera are *De Brouwer* (M904) and *Ommen* (M813). (RN)

9. Another group at sea in the English Channel: the minehunter *Nurton* (M1166), with *Marburg* (M1080), *Hoogezand* (M802) and *Knokke* (M931). The last, a Belgian ship, has been disposed of since the photograph was taken, but the others, British, West German and Dutch respectively, are still in service and will remain so throughout the 1980s. (RN)

10. Working together promotes efficient wartime operations. Each NATO navy learns to inter-operate, as illustrated here by the Dutch frigate *Isaac Sweers* (F814) and the Canadian frigate *Ottawa* (229) replenishing from USS *Savannah* (AOR-4).

11. In the Mediterranean, NATO has a multi-national, semi-permanent naval force known by the acronym NAVOCFORMED (Naval On-Call Force Mediterranean) which comes under the control of Allied Forces Southern Europe at Naples. This group is made up of frigates and destroyers but exercises with larger elements, such as the US Sixth Fleet (which is a NATO as well as a US command). Here the Greek destroyer *Tombasiz* (D215) takes fuel from RFA *Olna* (A123), as does the US strike carrier *Forrestal* (CV-59). (USN)

▲12 ▼13

12. Belgium's maritime contribution to NATO is concerned with mines countermeasures and the inshore patrol of the Benelux Channel area, although a construction programme in the middle of the 1970s has proved that the country does have the potential to provide a limited number of escorts. Four *Wielingen* Class frigates are in service (*Westhinder*, F913 is illustrated), which give the Royal Belgian Navy a stake in STANAVFORLANT as well as in STANAVFORCHAN. (RBN)

13. Also at Zeebrugge are the two command and support ships, which have duties connected with the large MCM effort of the Royal Belgian Navy. The newer of the two ships is the 2,685-ton *Zinnia* (A961), which is armed with three 40mm Bofors and carries a helicopter. (RBN)

14. The slightly smaller command and support ship *Godetia* (A960) was modified to operate an Alouette III light helicopter and can resupply sweep and minehunting gear to both coastal and inshore vessels at sea. This view shows the ship before a mid-life conversion which will replace the lifting gear and provide more comprehensive armaments. (RBN)

15. Immediately after the Second World War, the United States government provided aid for the formerly occupied countries to help re-establish their navies. Such aid, under the 'Offshore Account', included the provision of *Aggressive* Class minehunters such as *Van Haverbeke* (M902), seen here being followed into Ostend harbour by *A. F. Dufour* (M903). (RBN)

14▲ 15▼

▲16

16. The large number of *Adjutant* Class coastal minesweepers (MSC) which were supplied to Europe seem to have passed through Belgium before transfer to, amongst others, Norway and Greece. Several were retained by the RBN, including *Verviers* (M934). Note the NATO emblem on the funnel. (RBN)

17. The estuarine and shallow-water conditions around the Belgian coast, with its important entrances to inland waterways, have led to the RBN becoming extremely proficient in inshore MCM. Two operational squadrons, with a reserve of MSI craft, include *Ougrée* (M483). The large drum amidships is a minesweeping reel, used in conjunction with the various floats on deck. (RBN)

▼17

18. Canada has a responsibility for the North-Western Atlantic and Arctic island archipelago, which means that her anti-submarine warfare (ASW) forces must be strong. At present, these forces are led by four helicopter-carrying destroyers, known as 'DD-280s' or the *Iroquois* Class. Based at Halifax, Nova Scotia, the warships frequently make up the Canadian contribution to STANAVFOR-LANT. This is *Huron* (DD-281), leaving Halifax. (CF)

19. Although well endowed with ASW sensors and weapons, including two CH-124A Sea King helicopters (one is illustrated about to recover aboard *Algonquin*), the '280s' are lacking in anti-air defence, especially close-in. For duties with STANAVFORLANT, AAW is becoming more important because of the extended range of Soviet maritime strike aircraft. (CF)

▲20

▲21　▼22

23▲

20. The Royal Canadian Navy played an important part in the Second World War, becoming the third largest in the world by 1945; today, however, the numbers of warships are not so large, although the tasks are very similar. The Canadian Maritime Command (MARCOM) can expect to have to provide escorts for Atlantic passage to NATO countries in the event of war. Such an escort would include *Mackenzie* (261) of the class of that name. (CF)

21. Of similar design, but with ASW more in mind, the 'Improved *Restigouche*' Class are familiar in Eastern Atlantic and European waters. This photograph of *Terra Nova* (259) shows the destroyer before the fitting of the US ASROC rocket system aft (in place of the twin 76mm gun). The class is due to be replaced by a new Canadian frigate design in the mid-1980s. (CF)

22. The first class of warship to be designed in Canada after the Second World War comprised the *St. Laurent* frigates. They too will disappear from the active list by the late 1980s, even though they were modernized in the late 1960s to operate helicopters. This is *Saguenay* (206). (CF)

23. The first of the *St. Laurents* to be modified to take a more active role in the NATO Atlantic anti-submarine defences was *Assiniboine* (234), seen here operating a CH-124A Sea King from her flight deck, space for which was made by removing a twin 76mm gun and one of the Limbo ASW mortars. Note also the VDS (variable-depth sonar) on the stern, used for detecting submarines lurking below saline or temperature layers in the ocean. (CF)

24. Canada currently has a small submarine arm. The First Canadian Submarine Squadron, based at Halifax, is equipped with three British-built *Oberon* Class conventional submarines. These boats (*Ojibwa* is shown) are effective in continental shelf areas around Canada's Atlantic and Arctic coasts. The submarines no longer wear their pennant numbers on their fins but retain the maple leaf emblems. (CF)

24▼

▲ 25

25. Diving support for the Canadian Forces is provided by *Cormorant* (20) which was specially built for the task in 1978. This vessel was in the news in the early 1980s as one of the first non-US NATO warships to have female crew-members. (CF)

26. With the First and Fifth Destroyer Squadrons deployed in their

NATO and national roles, MARCOM has to support them with replenishment at sea. The first of three support vessels, known as AORs, was *Provider* (508), which carries oil and other products as well as three Sea King helicopters. (CF)

▼ 26

27▲

28▲

27. Denmark has a major contribution to make to NATO, guarding as she does an important exit route for Soviet warships in the event of war, and with Norway (and to a lesser extent West Germany), the Royal Danish Navy (RDN) has the role of preventing enemy use of the Kattegat and Skagerrak. There is also a role in the protection of the Faröe Islands and Greenland, both of which are Danish territory. For anti-surface vessel (ASV) roles the RDN is introducing the *Nils Juel* Class into service: this is the name ship on trials.

28. The new *Nils Juel* Class frigates are armed with eight Harpoon ASV missiles, eight Sea Sparrow launchers for anti-air warfare (AAW) and a single Compact 76mm gun. In due course, the ships will receive close-in missile defence, such is their vulnerability to air attack in any NATO war role. (RDN)

29. Anti-submarine work is not so important to the Danes. When the two *Peder Skram* Class vessels were completed, the planned fitting of Terne ASW launchers and ship-launched ASW torpedoes did not proceed because it was judged more important to fit the frigates for AAW with Sea Sparrow. This is the name-ship of the class, at sea during a NATO exercise. (RDN)

29▼

▲30 ▼31

32▲

30. At 1,970 tons, *Beskyttern* (F340) is an important patrol asset in an important NATO area. The ship carries a single Westland Lynx helicopter and has a hull specially strengthened to cope with ice floes in Arctic waters. (RDN)

31. The Faröes are considered to be an important location in the event of war, partly because they could provide bases for enemy attacks on Britain or Atlantic convoys. The RDN protects the area with *Hvidbjørnen* Class frigates (which are also used for North Sea survey work). This powerful vessel, well designed for its role, is the lead-ship of the class. (RDN)

32,33. The fact that Denmark is an archipelago, with shallow sea approaches in the Baltic, has led the RDN to acquire improved German Type 205 coastal diesel-electric submarines such as *Narhvalen* (S320, photograph 32) to replace the older *Delfinen* Class, built in the 1950s (photograph 33). Both types of submarine carry bow torpedo tubes for a range of 53cm torpedoes. (RDN)

34. Denmark has nearly fifty patrol craft in service, including fast missile craft (such as the *Willemoes* Class) built in Danish yards. The 260-ton *Norby* (P545) was commissioned in 1977 and will remain in service until the 1990s. (RDN)

33▼

34▼

▲ 35

▲ 36   ▼ 37

35. Designed to attack enemy shipping, particularly amphibious groups trying to make a landing and establish control of the Baltic approaches, the *Søløven* Class are built on Royal Navy *Brave* Class lines. This is *Søbjornen* (P512), at about 40kts. (RDN)

36,37. For duties further offshore or on patrols which could last for several days, the 170-ton *Daphne* Class, armed with depth charges and a single 40mm gun, are used. *Daphne* (photograph 36) was the first to be commissioned and *Rota* (37) the last. (RDN)

38. Looking rather like fishing boats, the *Agdlek* Class, such as *Tulugaq* (Y388) illustrated here, are a new type of large patrol craft designed specifically for the Greenland coast and able to endure the heavy weather there. (RDN)

39. The two *Maagen* Class craft operate closer to mainland Denmark. They displace 190 tons and are armed with only two 20mm Oerlikon cannon for 'police' work, but in war they would be charged with preventing raiding parties landing in small boats. *Maagen* is shown. (RDN)

40. With shallow seas all around it, the RDN has invested in both mines countermeasures vessels (MCMVs) and in minelayers: defensive mine-laying can often make up for a deficiency in numbers. This is *Møen* (N82) leaving Portsmouth after a courtesy visit; note the mine doors set into the stern. (Robin Walker)

38▲

39▲ 40▼

▲41

▲42 ▼43

41. The French *Marine* is one of two NATO navies with a full fixed-wing and conventional naval air element, and although France is not part of the NATO military planning structure during war it is expected that she would come to NATO's aid in the event of aggression by the Warsaw Pact. In that event, the French aircraft carriers would play an important part in the defence of the Mediterranean and Atlantic. Note the Étendard and Crusader air group overflying *Foch*. (ECPA)

42. Surely some of the most handsome of all warships are the *Tourville* Class of guided missile destroyers, illustrated here by *Tourville* herself entering Portsmouth harbour for one of the French Navy's infrequent visits. The ship is armed with Exocet (SSM), Crotale (SAM) and Malafon (ASW) systems, as well as two single 100mm mountings forward. Each of the three ships in the class carries two Lynx helicopters. (Robin Walker)

43. The French Atlantic Fleet, operating from Breton ports, has this 'one-off' anti-submarine frigate (designed as a destroyer) in commission. *Aconit* (D609), pictured here on a visit to London in 1980, is easily distinguishable from the later *Tourville* Class by the large air surveillance radar dome on the forward superstructure. The 305mm ASW mortar will probably be replaced with Exocet. (Robin Walker)

44. Pictured during joint exercises with the US Navy, the *Commandant Rivière* Class frigate *Enseigne de Vaisseau Henry* is over twenty years old but her weapon systems have been updated to include Exocet. Designed to carry staff officers and up to 80 troops, the frigates have been effective 'out of area' warships. (USN)

45. The highly successful A69-type frigates, designed and built by Lorient Naval Dockyard, have primarily a coastal anti-submarine role and would operate in support of NATO forces in the Channel, Atlantic and/or Mediterranean in the event of war. Besides the 375mm mortar launcher, the class are armed with tubes for ship-launched ASW torpedoes, self-defence being provided by Exocet and the single 100mm gun mounting forward. *Jean Moulin* is shown. (Robin Walker)

46. With the increasing risk of mine warfare being conducted against the NATO allies, the 1980s have seen the development of several new mines countermeasures vessels, including the so-called 'Tripartite' Class of minehunters. These vessels are being designed jointly by Belgium, the Netherlands and France, and the French lead-ship, *Ereidan* (M641), commissioned in 1982, is illustrated. The ships will act as parent vessels for the PAP unmanned minehunting system. (DTCN)

44▲

45▲ 46▼

▲47

47. The Federal German Navy (FGN) has developed from small beginnings in the mid-1950s to become one of the most powerful in Europe. Its main tasks are associated with Allied Forces Baltic Approaches, where its MCM and attack craft are concentrated. The ASW surface fleet is gaining modern equipment, however, and has a role to play in the defence of the North Sea and Channel. An important asset is the light cruiser-like training ship *Deutschland* (A59), seen here passing under Tower Bridge, London. (Robin Walker)

48. Three modern escorts along the lines of the *Charles F. Adams* Class were ordered from American yards in 1965, and they are known in FGN service as *Lütjens* Class destroyers. The first to be commissioned was *Lütjens* (D185) herself: note the gun armament,

▼48

which is scheduled to be modified in 1986, Harpoon surface-to-surface missiles (SSMs) replacing the after 127mm turret. (FGN)

49. Designed and built in Canadian yards for the important transatlantic anti-submarine threat to any re-supply of the Central Front of NATO, the '280' Class destroyers, like *Algonquin*, are miniature aircraft carriers which deploy two Sea King helicopters. (Canadian Forces)

50. Situated on the western side of the Atlantic, Halifax is an important NATO base for anti-ship duties and convoy support. In this photograph, the Canadian replenishment ship *Protecteur* is shown, with harbour tugs in the foreground. The 1st and 5th Destroyer Squadrons are also based at Halifax and are assigned to the NATO anti-submarine forces.

51. *Skeena* is one of the older helicopter-capable frigates of the Canadian Maritime Command and normally carries a single CH-124 Sea King helicopter. At the time this photograph was taken, the Sea King was disembarked at CFB Shearwater, just across Halifax Harbour.

52. The ability of NATO naval forces to remain at sea has been proved on countless exercises, and warships like these Canadian destroyers regularly make use of replenishment at sea (RAS) from supply ships such as *Protecteur* in their everyday duties. (Canadian Forces)

53. Supporting the various escorts, like *Halifax* (illustrated), are a number of specialized vessels, such as *Porte St. Jean* (180). In wartime, the latter would be used for gate duties, controlling anti-submarine booms across Halifax harbour.

◀51   52▲   53▼

▲ 54   ▼ 55

56▲

54. Although France is not a member of the NATO military council, her warships frequently exercise with those of other NATO navies. Here, the depot and support ship *Loire* is seen at Portsmouth during a visit to the mines countermeasures facility at *Vernon*. *Loire*'s primary role is to support the French Navy's minesweeper force.

55. In the late 1970s and early 1980s, NATO attempted to co-ordinate the design and fittings for new frigates, resulting in the 'Standard' type. This is the Dutch version, the *Kortenaer* Class: the lead ship is seen leaving Portland during operational sea training with the Royal Navy. (Author)

56. The *Hamburg* Class destroyers, built at Hamburg, were completed with an all-gun armament but have now been taken in hand for Exocet conversion; the missile battery, aft of the superstructure, is just visible in this view of *Hessen* (D184). (FGN)

57. The earlier West German destroyers and frigates are due to be replaced by a new class of 3,415-ton frigates not unlike the Dutch *Kortenaer*s; it is hoped that there will be eight hulls by 1986. The first Type 122, *Bremen* (F207), is shown. (FGN)

57▼

▲58

▲59　▼60

58. *Emden* is destined to pay off in the mid-1980s, but the name will be perpetuated by one of the new Type 122 frigates, demonstrating the esteem in which the FGN holds these warships. (FGN)

59. During two World Wars, the British (and, later, the Americans) were often at the mercy of a very professional German naval submarine arm; today, the twenty-four U-boats of the FGN are a key to NATO holding the Baltic Approaches in the event of war. The first class, the Type 205s, are torpedo-armed but also have a key minelaying role; small by 'super-power' concepts, they are ideal for shallow coastal waters. This is *U10* (pennant number S189). (FGN)

60. The Type 206 submarines are unique not only to NATO but to the world in having non-magnetic hulls. This great advantage is conferred by the use of special steels and also makes the boats useful for laying mines, which can be stowed in external carriers. This is *U24* (S173), photographed in a Baltic swell. (FGN)

61. During the Second World War the Germans were also noted for their design and development of the coastal patrol boat. Again, this expertise has not been lost, and about forty such craft are in service. They vary from the 732-ton corvettes of the *Thetis* Class, like *Najade* (P6054) . . .

62. . . . to the latest missile-armed fast attack craft, displacing half the corvette's tonnage yet carrying two 76mm guns and four Exocet missiles. They are capable of reaching over 35kts, as demonstrated by *S62* ('S'=*Schnellboot*), which has the pennant number P6112 to conform with NATO numbering systems. (FGN)

63. Most numerous of the FACs available to Baltic Approaches Command are the Type 148s, which were all built at Cherbourg and completed between 1972 and 1977. Needless to say, they are armed with the French Exocet system, in addition to Italian guns and with fittings from German yards – NATO co-operation in tangible form. *S52* (P6152) was completed in 1974 and should remain in service until 1990. (FGN)

61▲

62▲   63▼

▲64

64. Shallow seas mean mine warfare – again, a German special-ization which has led to the development of several types of MCMV. Coastal craft with several days' endurance are represented by the *Schütze* Class, which can act as sweepers, hunters or guidance ships for the Troika remotely controlled underwater vehicle. *Konstanz* (M1081) is illustrated. (FGN)

65. Inshore, the minesweepers take on the appearance of Second World War R-boats. The *Ariadne* Class were in fact originally patrol vessels but were later refitted to form the Third Mines Counter Measures Squadron. *Vineta* is shown wearing M2665, but she has now been renumbered M2652. (FGN)

▼65

66▲

66. With so many small craft at sea, the FGN has to provide a comprehensive depot ship programme, and *Lüneburg* (A1411) is one of over a dozen such vessels which support the FAC. She has full facilities for maintaining the Exocet missiles of both patrol boats and larger craft. (FGN)

67. The *Rhein* Class of support ships have been modified to deal with the needs of submarines, attack craft and, in the case of *Mosel* (A67), minesweepers. In the event of war, they would provide bases which could be mobile and yet possess all the facilities necessary for sustained operations. (FGN)

67▼

▲68   ▼69

68. Greece has a key position on NATO's Southern Flank and at the end of the Mediterranean Sea which is troubled by strife and conflict, and it is therefore not surprising that the Hellenic Navy (HN) has built up a balanced force over the last two decades. Leading the naval forces are several former USN destroyers, such as *Sachtouris* (D214), a former *Gearing* (FRAM I) Class warship transferred in 1973. (HN)

69. Greece has purchased a *Kortenaer* Class 'Standard' frigate from the Netherlands, with the intention of building three more in home yards. The first of the class has been named *Elli* (F450) and was originally destined for the Dutch Navy. Instead of carrying the Westland Navy Lynx as do the Dutch frigates, *Elli* and her sister-ships will be equipped with Agusta Bell 212 helicopters, two of which can be accommodated. (HN)

70. The Aegean Islands would provide an interesting hunting ground for submarines in the event of war, especially because of the forced passage of Soviet warships from the Black Sea Fleet. Greece turned to Germany for her new boats, Type 209s, which are known as the *Glavkos* Class; each boat has an endurance of more than fifty days. (HN)

71. In the same way as the Norwegian and the Baltic NATO navies, the Hellenic Navy has sound operational reasons for employing fast attack craft, especially missile boats. There are currently nearly forty light attack craft on strength, a typical example being *Skorpios* (P55), a former West German *Jaguar* Class boat armed with Exocet and 40mm Bofors guns. (HN)

▲72 ▼73

72. The Italians have now joined the 'carrier club' with a 13,370-tonne through-deck cruiser capable of operating STOVL aircraft like the Sea Harrier but currently planned to embark sixteen Sea King helicopters only. The ship, named after that great Italian Giuseppe Garibaldi, was launched in June 1983 and is expected to be operational in 1985. The carrier is heavily armed with anti-air and anti-surface guided weapons and ASW torpedoes. It is a welcome addition to the NATO naval forces in the Mediterranean. (ItN)

73. Before the advent of the *Giuseppe Garibaldi*, Italian naval air units operated from a line of very successful helicopter-cruisers/destroyers like *Caio Duilio* (C554), seen here with Terrier SAMs on the forward launcher. (ItN)

74. *Andrea Doria* (C553) is the name-ship of the two cruiser classes which were designed in the late 1950s and will be replaced by *Garibaldi* in 1985. They are well armed, with provision for ship-launched ASW torpedoes and eight 76mm guns; the latter, fully automatic for anti-aircraft defence, may not be ideal for close-in defence against sea skimming missiles, and so their life is limited in a NATO navy of the 1980s. (ItN)

75. NATO currently has too few frigates, but Italy has gone some way to provide good ASW escorts, such as the new *Maestrale* Class of 3,000 tons. This is the name-ship, which will be joined by eight more in the period 1984–85. Otomat Mk. 2 and Albatros/ Aspide guided missiles are mounted, as well as guns and torpedoes. (ItN)

74▲   75▼

▲76

76. The standard ASW frigate of the Italian Navy is the *Lupo* Class; *Sagittario* (F565) is illustrated, with her Agusta-Bell 212 on deck. Note also the twin Dardo 40mm guns in the turret abreast the hangar. (ItN)

77. After the Second World War, the United States began to assist in the build-up of friendly navies in Europe. One programme was the construction of three anti-submarine frigates known as the *Centauro* Class. The last of these vessels to be laid down was *Cigno* (F555), seen here at about half her 25kts operational speed. (ItN)

78. After brief experiments with helicopters carried in refitted frigates, the Italian Navy built two *Alpino* Class ships, which will remain in service until the end of the decade. *Carabiniere* has a single mortar and ship-launched ASW torpedoes as well as the successful AB 212 helicopter. Anti-air and anti-surface vessel defence is provided by 40mm and 127mm guns respectively. (ItN)

79. The Italians operate corvettes for coastal escort work, *Umberto Grosso* (F541) being one of four 1960s-vintage vessels due to be supplemented by six further corvettes in 1988–90. These warships are lightly armed with basic ASW weapons and two 76mm guns, but are effective in their role. (ItN)

▼77

78▲ 79▼

▲80 ▼81

80. Submarines and all forms of undersea warfare are an Italian forte, and the NATO ASW Research Centre is located at La Spezia, indicating the Alliance's faith in Italian expertise. Four *Enrico Toti* Class boats were ordered after the Second World War, including *Lazzaro Mocenigo* (S514), which commissioned in 1969. The class are armed with eight 53cm torpedoes and have an endurance of about 35 days.

81. The larger and more recent *Nazario Sauro* Class have longer range and more firepower and are capable of remaining on patrol for 45 days: they can travel 12,500nm dived, with occasional 'snorting' to run the diesels to charge the batteries. The name-boat (S518) is shown. (ItN)

82. Part of the undersea warfare contribution to NATO is the Italian Navy's MCM flotilla, which includes 25 coastal minesweepers like *Larice* (M5510), which was American-built. A class of new MCMVs has been ordered as part of the continued NATO programme against the possible mining of important seaways and choke-points. (ItN)

83. Italy has a long coast line, one side of which faces the Balkans and has many inlets and islands to patrol and protect. This is the hunting ground of the fast attack craft (FAC). The other coast is equally long and is also the operating area for patrol boats like the 200-ton *Lampo* (P491), seen here in a gunboat role with three 40mm guns. For torpedo-boat operations, the craft can be converted to carry two 53cm torpedoes and two 40mm Bofors. (ItN)

84. Any nation with a large number of escorts at sea, especially if they have a helicopter complement, needs replenishment ships capable of carrying fuel, aviation spirit and freight. The Italian Navy ordered two such tankers in the early 1970s; this is the first, *Stromboli* (A5327). (ItN)

82▲

83▲   84▼

▲85　▼86

87▲

85. The *Kortenaer* Class ships of the Royal Netherlands Navy, like *Philips Van Almonde* (F823), are considered to be more than just frigates – they are integrated weapons systems which contribute greatly to the NATO Atlantic forces. Their primary role is ASW, but they have good ASV and AAW capabilities as well. (RN)

86. Part of the *Kortenaers*' ASW equipment is the Westland SH-14 Lynx helicopter, seen here flying over *Van Kinsbergen* (F809) during exercises in the North Sea. Note the ship's Sea Sparrow canister launchers, immediately forward of the bridge, and the 76mm gun. (RNethN)

87. The highly successful British *Leander* Class general-purpose frigates were introduced to the Royal Netherlands Navy in the late 1960s and have recently been modernized to give them viability through to the 1990s. *Van Speyk* (F802) was the first to undergo refit, which included the replacement of the original 114mm gun with a quick-firing 76mm type and the replacement of the mortar with ASW torpedo tubes. (RNethN)

88. Flagship roles are usually undertaken by one of the two *Tromp* Class frigates, warships which are generally rated as destroyers by other navies. This is *Tromp* (F801), known as 'Kojak' to the Fleet because of the distinctive HSA 3-D radome towering above the bridge. (RNethN)

88▼

89. The helicopter is still a key weapon in the fight against submarines which have the potential of cutting the Netherlands' and NATO's sea trade links with the rest of the world. This view shows a Lynx recovering aboard *Kortenaer* in the North Sea. (RNethN)

90. Although small by NATO standards, the Royal Belgian Navy has been steadily improving its equipment over the last ten years.

This is *Wandelaar*, one of a class of anti-submarine frigates designed to work in the North Sea; it is pictured at its base at Zeebrugge.

91. To support the mines countermeasures flotilla of the Royal Belgian Navy, the support depot ship *Godetia* has been in commission since 1966 and will probably remain in service until 1996. The ship also has a cadet training role.

◀92

92. The West German schoolship *Deutschland*, seen alongside the museum ship *Belfast*, during a courtesy visit to the Pool of London.
93. STANAVFORCHAN, the NATO mines countermeasures force, regularly pays courtesy visits to member nations, as well as exercising in their roles. The Belgian MCMV *Breybel* (M906) is

93▲

pictured with the Federal German Navy's *Paderborn* in the Pool of London on a visit to Great Britain. (Author)
94. Alongside in the Pool of London are FGNS *Lindau* (M1072) with the British MCMV *Hubberston* (M1147) during a courtesy visit by STANAVFORCHAN. (Author)

94▼

▲95 ▼96

95. NATO's only real hope of lasting security in the 1980s and beyond lies with co-operation between military and political forces; these Dutch and British warships exercising in the English Channel give a clear example of such co-operation. *Groningen* (nearest) is being phased out of service, but the *Leander* Class frigate and *Birmingham* (right) will remain active until at least 1990. (Author)
96. The United States Navy is building new nuclear-powered attack submarines to counter the continued growth in numbers of Soviet ballistic and attack types. This is the launch of the SSN *Olympia* in 1983; by 1985, the boat had joined the Atlantic Fleet. Like the Royal Navy (the only other NATO navy with SSNs), the US Navy

has developed its SSNs as an élite force.
97. An underway replenishment group (URG) steams during a RAS(L) for fuel. *Poolster* replenishes *Van Kinsbergen* (F809) and, right, *Banckert* (F810); astern is a third frigate of the same class. (RNethN)
98. The Netherlands has acquired two fast tankers for NEF support operations (including the replenishment of weapons) and to transport small groups of marines in an emergency. Both *Poolster* Class ships carry female members of crew. This is *Zuiderkruis* (A832), the second unit, which will be joined by a third in the mid-1980s. (RNethN)

▲99   ▼100

101▲

99. The best anti-submarine weapon is another submarine. This maxim is well understood in the Dutch Navy, which currently operates six SSK (conventional) boats and has two more on order. The latest are two *Zwaardvis* Class boats, which have a hull form similar to that of a nuclear-powered submarine. *Zwaardvis* (S806) is seen here, entering Portsmouth. (RN)

100. For fisheries protection and other general duties, the Dutch have a small number of patrol craft: *Bulgia* (P803) is seen here at Flushing, the secondary naval base, alongside a squadron of shallow-draught minesweepers of the *Van Straelen* Class, now stricken. (Fred J. Bachofner)

101. The threat of mining is taken very seriously by the Dutch government, and the Navy contributes craft to STANAVFORCHAN and mans the Benelux Channel Command headquarters of NATO. Part of the effort consists of a class of eighteen coastal minesweepers, like *Drachten* (M812).

102. The new *Alkmaar* Class has been designed for the 1980s, in a co-operative venture with the Belgian and French Navies. The vessels have sophisticated electronics, including data-processing and position-keeping, as well as the latest search and classification gear. The first of the class is *Alkmaar* (M850) herself and she began trials in 1982; fourteen more units will follow. (RNethN)

102▼

▲103 ▼104

105▲

106▲

103. The recently modified *Oslo* Class frigates, built in middle 1960s as part of the continuing NATO ASW effort, are the pride of the Royal Norwegian Navy (RNN). *Narvik* (F304) was the third of five units, which were completed with Arctic and Norwegian Sea conditions in mind. The armament of this 1,745-ton ship includes two triple Mk.32 torpedo tubes and a Terne ASW rocket launcher. (Forsvarets)
104. The *Oslos* are the largest surface combat ships in the RNN and one unit is often attached to STANAVFORLANT. These two frigates, *Stavanger* and *Oslo* (right), were photographed shortly after a NATO exercise designed to test the Alliance's preparedness in the North Sea and Baltic Approaches. (RN)
105. At about the same time as the *Oslos* were ordered, the Norwegian government progressed to the design of a cheaper and smaller ASW vessel of the corvette type. Only two *Sleipner* Class

vessels were built, including the name-ship, seen here on coastal patrol. (Forsvarets)
106. The fjord coast of Norway, with its many islands, lends itself to operations by fast attack craft, and the RNN has developed complex and effective tactics for both missile-armed and gun-equipped craft. *Snögg* (P980) is the lead-boat of a class of six, all commissioned in 1970–71. They carry Penguin missiles and 21in (53cm) torpedo tubes, as well as a single 40mm Bofors gun. (Forsvarets)
107. Norway also maintains a substantial and very effective Coast Guard service for the patrol of fishing grounds and, more importantly, the protection of oil platforms in the North Sea. For this new role, which began in 1977, the Navy has taken delivery of three new cutters, the first being *Nordkapp* (W320). These vessels are armed and carry Lynx helicopters. (Plessey)

107▼

108. The twenty *Storm* Class FACs have the same hull as the *Snögg*s but are more heavily armed with missiles, carrying six single launchers and no torpedo tubes. The missiles were added in 1970, complementing the existing single 76mm (forward) and 40mm Bofors guns. (Forsvarets)

109. The coast of Norway, said to be the longest in world if every bay, fjord and island is counted, lends itself to mining, and the country is thought to have planned or dormant defensive mines to protect certain key installations and coastal passages. To lay and maintain these fields, two specialist 400-mine craft have been built; this is the second, *Vale* (N53), which was completed in 1978. (Forsvarets)

110. Should the enemy lay its own mines, then the job of clearing them would lie with the ten specialist minesweepers of the RNN. Five are former US Navy *Falcon* Class MCMVs, some previously in service with Belgium, and five were built in Norway, including *Utla* (M334), seen here entering Portsmouth with the Queen's Harbourmaster's launch in attendance. (RN)

▲108   ▼109

▲111

111. Having essentially a coastal navy and a coastal role in NATO, Norway has developed, with West German and American assistance, a class of deep-diving conventional coastal submarines. The Type 207s, typified by *Skoplen* (S306), have an eighteen-man crew and are probably tasked with preventing an enemy amphibious force and its support elements from landing on Norwegian territory. (Forsvarets)

112. The coastal submarines and FACs of the RNN are supported by a single 2,500-ton depot ship, *Horten* (A530), which was designed specifically for Arctic conditions. The vessel is armed with a single 40mm Bofors gun and has a helicopter deck. (Forsvarets)

113. Amongst the most effective ships in the Portuguese Navy (PN) are the four *Comandante João Belo* Class frigates of 2,250 tons. *Comandante Sacadura Cabral* (F483), launched in 1968, is shown. (Mike Lennon)

114. Based on the USN's *Dealey* Class, the three frigates of the *Almirante Pereira Da Silva* Class are due for modernization, having been launched nearly twenty years ago. Photographed sailing in home waters is the name-ship of the class (F472). (PN)

115. Built in Spanish yards, the *Baptista de Andrade* Class frigates were originally thought to be destined for the Colombian Navy, but instead have remained in Portuguese service. *Afonso Cerqueira* (F488) still awaits the proposed MM38 Exocet fit. (PN)

▼112

113▲

114▲ 115▼

▲116 ▼117

118▲

116. One of several navies to buy the French 1,000-ton *Daphne* Class conventional coastal submarine, the Portuguese Navy received three between 1967 and 1969. The first was *Albacora* (S163), seen here on a windless day and barely making steerage way. (PN)

117. The Portuguese Navy is primarily anti-submarine in nature, as shown by the equipment aboard *Almirante Magalhães Corrêa* (F474), which includes not only Bofors ASW rockets (under the bridge) but also two sets of triple-barrelled ASW torpedo tubes (amidships) and the American SQA-10A variable-depth sonar at the stern. (Mike Lennon)

118. The most recent member of NATO, although not yet of the integrated command structure, is Spain. A nation with a long maritime tradition, she has a well-balanced navy which will soon include *Principe de Asturias*, an aircraft carrier of 14,700 tons being built to replace the present light helicopter carrier *Dedalo* (shown). Both ships are of American design. (Mike Lennon)

119. The older, Second World War-built warships of the Spanish Navy are now being phased out. *Almirante Fernandez* (D22) has already gone and will be followed by the rest of the *Fletcher* Class destroyers transferred to Spain in 1972. (Mike Lennon)

119▼

▲120

120. When the Spanish government cancelled an order for British *Leander* Class frigates in 1962, they built instead, with considerable US assistance, a class of five 'F70' frigates, known as the *Baléares* Class, after the lead-ship. Although similar to the USN's *Knox* Class, these warships have many Spanish features and lack helicopter facilities. (Mike Lennon)

121. Armed with Harpoon and Sea Sparrow, the 'F30' (*Descubierta*) Class frigates are the latest Spanish surface combat ships to enter service. *Infante Elena* (F33), named after one of the King's daughters, is a corvette in Spanish eyes and was commissioned into service in 1979. (Mike Lennon)

122. One of the assets which Spanish membership of NATO brings the Alliance is a powerful amphibious capability, which includes *Galicia* (formerly USS *San Marcos*), a 9,375-ton landing ship dock (LSD) which can accommodate three large landing craft and eleven helicopters. (Mike Lennon)

123. Wooden-hulled minesweepers such as *Odiel* (M26), seen here with her old hull number, are important members of the Spanish MCM effort. As yet, these forces have not integrated with STANAVFORCHAN nor with any other NATO command, but their commonality of equipment should make them compatible. (Mike Lennon)

▼121

122▲ 123▼

▲124 ▼125

124. The Turkish Navy (TN) has an important role to play in safeguarding the eastern Mediterranean Sea and the passage through the Dardanelles from the Black Sea. This latter sea lane is guarded by light forces using fast missile craft like *Dogan*, the lead-boat of the *Lürssen* Class. The main armament is the Harpoon anti-ship missile. (TN)

125. The *Fletcher* Class destroyers proved very successful in the Pacific Ocean during the Second World War and it is therefore not surprising that several NATO navies were equipped with warships of the class transferred from the USN. This is the destroyer *Istanbul* (formerly *Clarence K. Bronson*), which was commissioned into the Turkish Navy in January 1967. (TN)

126. In the Mediterranean, the Turkish Navy operates several types of escort, including the FRAM II-modified *Allen M. Sumner* Class destroyer *Zafer*, formerly the USN's *Hugh Purvis*, commissioned in 1945. (TN)

126 ▶

◀127
128▲

127. The Royal Navy is committed to provide NATO with warships to screen the re-supply routes from North America from enemy submarines, to clear mines in the English Channel and North Sea, to protect vital shipping with escorts, to reinforce the Northern Flank and to perform a number of other related tasks. The largest RN warships now in commission are the *Invincible* Class. Completed early in order to relieve her sister-ship *Invincible*, the second of the class, *Illustrious*, joined the Fleet in 1982; she is pictured here at the end of the NATO exercise 'Autumn Train', with Sea King HAS.5 helicopters and Sea Harrier FRS.1 fighters spotted on deck. (HMS *Illustrious*)

128. The lynch-pin of the Northern Flank reinforcement plan is the assault ship *Fearless* (seen here off Norway in 1983) and her sister-ship *Intrepid*. Both can carry helicopters, landing craft and a Royal Marine Commando. They have Seacat SAMs and 40mm Bofors for self-protection. (Author)

129. A key role in peacetime is the shadowing of Soviet warships in the Atlantic Ocean, North Sea and Norwegian Sea. This photograph was taken in 1980 when the *Leander* Class frigate *Juno* (F52), flagship of STANAVFORLANT, met the Soviet carrier *Kiev* in the Arctic Circle. (NATO)

129▼

▲130

▲131 ▼132

130. Amongst the units assigned to, dedicated to or, in the event of war, expected to operate under SACLANT are the British conventional submarines. *Onyx* is illustrated.

131. *Brilliant*, one of the Royal Navy's Type 22 *Broadsword* Class ASW frigates. Eight such ships were designed; they were the first ships in RN service to lack a gun armament, but Batch III Type 22s will have a single gun. (Robin Walker)

132. The *Leander* Class frigates have, in their several guises, been in the front line of the British commitment to NATO maritime power for nearly two decades. This is *Minerva*, leaving Portsmouth for a

refit which will make her even more effective for NATO work in the 1980s. (Robin Walker)

133. As a result of the Falklands War, several older RN frigates, kept in the Standby Squadron for just such an eventuality, were returned to service to maintain the NATO commitment. *Falmouth* (F113) was one such warship. (RN)

134. The RN has been building up its MCMV support for NATO in recent years, in the face of continuing Warsaw Pact dominance in this form of maritime warfare. This is the first of the new GRP-hulled *Hunt* Class vessels, *Brecon* (M29). (RN)

▲135 ▼136

135. The United States Navy's aircraft carriers make up the backbone of NATO's Striking Fleet, a command subordinate to SACLANT. The carrier can project power and deterrent force in every theatre. *Dwight D. Eisenhower* (CVN-69) is shown here, operating in the Mediterranean in support of Allied Forces Southern Europe. (NATO)

136. The packed deck of a nuclear-powered carrier includes ASW, AAW and electronic warfare and intelligence gathering aircraft. For forces which are numerically inferior to a potential enemy, the advantages of mobile air power are enormous. This is *Dwight D. Eisenhower* again, lying off Portsmouth during the NATO autumn exercise season. (RN)

137. To protect the aircraft carrier forces, the US Navy has developed a number of fast and powerful nuclear-powered guided missile cruisers, of which *California* (CGN-36) is an example. These ships are engaged mainly in the detection of threats and the direction of supporting combat air patrols, and their armament includes Harpoon (SSM), Standard (SAM) and ASROC (ASW).

138. Smaller, less expensive escorts deployed with NATO forces include the ASW frigates of the *Garcia* Class, such as *Sample* (FF-1048), which is larger and better equipped for ASW than many destroyers. She is seen here during ASW trials. (Lockheed)

138▼

▲139

139. The ubiquitous *Knox* Class frigates can be seen in most NATO theatres. They are equipped with the Kaman Seasprite LAMPS I helicopter and with Sea Sparrow and Harpoon missiles. This is *Elmer Montgomery* (FF-1082), leaving Southampton after a courtesy visit in 1982. (Robin Walker)

140. Amphibious forces for reinforcement landings on the Northern and Southern Flanks are backed substantially by the US Navy and the US Marine Corps. This rare picture of a USN Seal Team member was taken during recent combined amphibious exercises in Turkey; in the background is a landing craft utility, *LCU-1610*. (NATO)

141. The USN has built five *Tarawa* Class specialist amphibious

assault ships, of which two (including *Saipan*, illustrated) are based with the Atlantic Fleet. They are beautiful ships with two complete hangar decks, a docking well and command facilities. Self-contained defence measures include Sea Sparrow missiles and close in weapons. (USN)

142,143. (Overleaf) Other specialist vessels assigned to support NATO landing operations include the tank landing ship *Sumter* (LST-1181) and the dock landing ship *Fort Snelling* (LSD-30). These warships would play a major role in any preventative or reinforcement landings that might be required, from Norway to Turkey. (RN)

141▶

▼140

▲142 ▼143